NORMA.

MAKE
AMERICA
HOPE
AGAIN

A PLAN TO WIN IN DIVERSITY & INCLUSION
FOR CORPORATE AMERICA

outskirts
press

Outskirts Press, Inc.
http://www.outskirtspress.com

ISBN: 978-1-4327-7114-0

PRINTED IN THE UNITED STATES OF AMERICA

This book is dedicated to my parents, Lindsey Fleming Sr. and Laura D. Fleming. And, my sister and brothers; Laura E., Joseph Davis, Lindsey Jr., and Anthony M. Fleming.

TABLE OF CONTENTS

MY NAME IS Norman P. Fleming. I act as an employee at the Sankofa Times Company (a fictional publication company) for ten years. What follows in this memoir are my experiences as a person of color: Bi-racial; Belizean Hispanic and African American male. The primary purpose of my story is to provide real-world lessons learned and leading practices on diversity & inclusion for People of Color (POC). After you read my book, I pray that we can work together to "**Make America Hope Again**."

This fictional company has an account of characters that do not exist in a corporation. This book should be viewed as a learning platform with a vision to achieve 100% inclusion for all races in corporate America. My definition of people of color are all races; White-LGBTQs/Disabled, African American, Hispanic, Asian, Native Indian, and Bi-Racial or Other. As a USA citizen, I value, respect and love all European races outlined in my memoir:

Italian, Irish, Australian, German, Polish, Russian, and Other.

After the recent hate outrage in Charlottesville, Virginia, it is time for our country to come together again as one race; The United States of America race.

A quote from Nelson Mandela's 1994 autobiography, "Long Walk to Freedom," read, *"No one is born hating another person because of the color of his skin or his background or his religion. People must learn to hate, and if they can learn to hate, they can be taught to love, for love comes more naturally to the human heart than its opposite."*

AFTER BEING EMPLOYED with the Sankofa Times Company, a Fortune 100 Company, for more than ten years, I've concluded that racial discrimination and limiting career opportunities for People of Color (POC) has been a common practice across corporate America. As a dark-skinned male, I've personally been discriminated against and restricted in career opportunities by the "glass ceiling" metaphor during various periods at the Sankofa Times.

The Sankofa Times preserves an environment that intentionally limits and prevents People of Color from reaching their full career potential unless you're categorized as "white male," "token," or a "safe" employee. I will expound on the definition of "safe" and "token" later in this book.

The "glass ceiling" refers to invisible, artificial barriers that prevent qualified individuals from advancing within their organization and reaching their full potential. The term originally described the point beyond which minority managers and executives, particularly African Americans, were not promoted. In 2017, it is evident that ceilings and walls still exist throughout most workplaces for People of Color and women. These barriers are a result of institutional and psychological practices which limit the advancement and mobility opportunities of men and women of diverse racial and ethnic backgrounds. Even White employees that have disabilities and are known as LGBTQs are under the same barriers.

At the Sankofa Times, the professional job classification (1 to 22) for full-time employment base salaries starts at grade 12 (entry-level college educated) and ends at grade 22 (vice president) for professional employees. The glass ceiling for People of Color is the professional grade 18 level; equivalent to director-level role in most industries or sectors. However, a very small percentage of People of Color are ever hired or promoted above the job grade 15 level (individual contributor level).

The Sankofa Times Company (corporate) has a policy which reflects their beliefs in equal employment opportunities for all, regardless of race, color, religion, sex, national origin, age, disability or any other legally protected classification. It is the company's policy to hire and promote the most qualified applicants to comply with all federal, state and local equal employment opportunity laws. This policy governs employment and all the company's terms and conditions of employment, including, but not limited to, policies and practices affecting recruitment, recruitment advertising, hiring, promotions, demotion, transfers, reclassification, selection of training, compensation, benefits, company sponsored educational programs and any other aspect of employment.

Unfortunately, the Sankofa Times has done a very poor job in developing and retaining high potential (i.e., HiPo) **People of Color Professionals (i.e., POCs)**. POCs have been treated unequally in promotions, succession planning, selection for high visible projects, professional training, and compensation.

What follows in this book is a 10-year chronology that represents my experience of adverse patterns and practices that are invisible (subtle). This has caused POCs undue stress, depression, unfair terminations, long-term career disappointments and early employment separations. Conversely, the book highlights a decade of leading practices for POCs to counter these adverse conditions and bring their authentic best in a **"Plan to Win in Diversity and Inclusion"** for corporate America.

YEAR 1
(2008)

AS A PROFESSIONAL with one year of work experience in retail and a bachelor of science degree in management, I was hired as a field service account coordinator at the Sankofa Times Newspaper Company in 2008. I was interviewed by senior human resources supervisor, Jim Boone (white male), city home delivery manager, Ron McDonald (white male, grade 17 - who grew up in Chicago's most segregated White-only neighborhood), and field training and development manager, Earl Floyd (African American male, grade 16 – former major league baseball player).

I accepted the entry-level management position, job grade 12 in the publication department. My starting salary was $22,100 annually.

Table 1.0

The minimum in a job grade 12 was $19,656. Midpoint was $24,570. Maximum salary for my grade was $29,484.

I reported to an African American male, Earl Floyd. Mr. Floyd was intimidating, a tall person (6'5"), muscular and had a very deep voice. He was focused, but trustworthy and nurturing. You could tell that he was an athlete that had played in a professional sport. I felt that I could trust him.

This was a period in which the publication department was recruiting POC employees to convert their distributor distribution network to independent delivery agents. The company's number one strategic program was called the 2008 agent conversion. There were four distinct publication management functions in the department: city home delivery (Chicago – delivery of newspapers to residential homes), city street sales (Chicago – delivery of newspapers to retail or commercial outlets), suburban publication (local Chicago counties outside of Cook county– delivery of newspapers to homes and retail outlets), and national publication (USA states and counties outside of the Chicago 9-county area - delivery of newspapers to homes and retail outlets).

Field service account coordinators were job grade 12, field service account managers were job grade 13, division managers were job grade 15, field training and development managers were job grade 16, field systems managers were job grade 16, city operations managers were job grade 16, national operations and transition managers were job grade 16, regional sales managers were job grade 17 and directors were job grade 18 and above. These classifications still exist as of 2017.

The professional grade 16 level in the publication department represented the 1st line of supervision for people management responsibilities. The job grade normally encompassed responsibilities managing entry-level Sankofa Times employees and the management of financial budgets. These responsibilities were not provided to a job grade 15 and below; for example, division manager positions or other individual contributor field management positions.

The city home delivery department encompassing the city of Chicago market had 12 (43%) African American coordinators, 3 (10%) Hispanic coordinators, 13 (47%) White coordinators. The department was well balanced with POCs for the predominantly minority market. However, the first three coordinators promoted to division manager positions (grade 15) in 2008 were white males.

The city street sales department encompassing the Chicago single copy market had one African American coordinator and no Hispanic or Asian coordinators. The suburban publication department encompassing all of the suburban towns within Chicago's 9-county market had six African American coordinators and no Hispanic or Asian coordinators. The suburban department had 150%

more manager/professionals than the city home delivery department. The national publication department had no POC professionals.

Later on in the year, two publication management trainees were hired, one white male (grade 12) and one African American male (grade 12). The company's management trainee program was a 2-year leadership rotation program. The program was designed for college graduates. It provided high profile rotational leadership opportunities for the trainee to learn and work in every business function across the entire publication department. Only high-potential college graduates were hired into this program.

My job scope was very narrow; it only focused on learning publication activities in one business function, the city home delivery department; which did not include single copy operations. My primary job was to manage open publication accounts. This entailed starting work at 2:00 am in the morning six days a week, and making sure that the newspapers were delivered by the adult motor route drivers. If a driver did not come in to deliver a route, then normally I would have to deliver the newspaper route. It was obvious that management did not want white males exposed to delivering routes in African American or Hispanic neighborhoods.

After the first three months in my position, I received positive feedback on my performance from my immediate supervisor, Earl Floyd. I applied for a division manager position, job grade 15 after three months on the job. The White hiring manager, Ron McDonald, selected Jerry Trump (white male). I was told that I did not have enough publication experience to be selected for the role. Incidentally, Jerry did not have a college degree, but I did. A division manager position required a college degree or 7+ years of equivalent work experience. Jerry started in the company only three months before I did.

Ron McDonald was a thin-skinned emotional leader. He had red hair, a proud Irish heritage, and was a micro-manager. He called his direct reports every morning at 6:30 am to make sure they were in the office.

The company's annual performance rating scale reflected 1=Unsatisfactory, 2=Marginal, 3=Satisfactory, 4=Above Average, 5= Exceptional.

After six months in the company (August 2008), my performance was rated "satisfactory." I received a 5% increase in my annual salary. Our mid-year and annual performance ratings were normally based on three performance goals, 1. customer service, 2. publication growth and 3. collection results. I supervised independent contractors, i.e., motor route drivers, newspaper stuffers, and delivery agents. The Chicago African American markets had the worst service and collection metrics due to external factors such as poverty, crime, and high agent/ driver turnover.

There were two African American city home delivery division managers in the function: June Smith and Terry Payton. They were both responsible for the South side of Chicago. A Hispanic division manager was responsible for the West side of Chicago. The white male division managers had the best markets in Chicago. Senior management valued performance based on two critical priorities: profitable publication growth and customer service. The minority markets represented the lowest publication revenue increases and worst customer service results. The four White division managers had the best performing P/L markets.

In December, I applied for the district sales manager (a promotion) position in the city streets sales department. City Streets Sales Manager Angry Young, (white male) interviewed me for the position. Although I felt that the interview went well, I was not selected for the position. This is the second position I applied for in one year.

My immediate manager, Earl Floyd, won the annual Sankofa Company President's Award for his performance in 2008. This is the highest award in the department. Out of 30+ employees recognized, POCs Doug Williams (African American male) and Angela Clark (African American female) also won "Special Recognition" awards for their performance. Clarence Thomas (African American male, grade 17) was the only African American in the past 100 years to win the President's award prior to Earl. Clarence won the award twice in the past decade. Normally, when an employee wins the President's Award, there is a higher probability to break the glass ceiling.

FY2008 CONCLUSIONS – LESSONS LEARNED:

- Corporate America: People of color should be assigned to any market that requires the best and brightest talent. Talent wins in markets, not race. Also, recognizing diverse talent in employee recognition programs is a good practice. Employees notice when talent is recognized more than personal or political relationships.

- People of Color: In your first year on the job, this is a critical time to build your brand. Performance matters and making sure you hit all your goals is critical. Collaborating with colleagues, demonstrating a positive attitude, exceeding expectations, and embracing change are key performance attributes.

YEAR 2
(2009)

IN YEAR TWO of employment, I realized that POCs, including myself, were always responsible for the West side and South side of Chicago. White males were always given assignments in the Loop, Goldcoast and non-minority markets. I was categorized as one of the few POC leaders and one of the best field service coordinators in Earl's area. However, my brand was temporarily tarnished in my 2nd year because of several verbal conflicts I had with white division managers; Mike Albert (grade 15), Dick Young (grade 15) and field service manager Mary Jane (grade 16). Earl warned me that they were threatened by me because of my confidence, drive for perfection, and performance; and it was rare for POCs to stand up to their condescending and entitled ways.

For example, when I did not fill the company truck with gas (I did not know that we had a fuel account and I did not know anything about the truck policy), Mike Albert called me on the phone and cursed me out, used demeaning and insulting words (called me stupid and lazy) against me. I told him that he was rude and unprofessional and I would not accept his verbal abuse. I reported the incident to Earl. At that time, I represented an aberration. POC employees were supposed to be docile and passive aggressive. I learned that you should never challenge a white employee.

Field Service Account Coordinator Will Smith (African American) was perceived as this type of employee. He received special treatment and more opportunities to learn the business than I did. Will knew how to smile, laugh, and play the political game. He was skinny, dressed conservative, and looked like a nerd.

The White management team labeled him as "safe." Mary Jane appointed him to a publications management trainee position (lateral move, grade 12) in late 2008.

In addition, it was very clear to me that you did not have any chance of being successful in the publication department unless you were promoted to a division manager position (grade 15). The division manager position was the "first level" management P/L position that positioned your career for long-term senior management success.

Furthermore, Earl fired African American field account manager, Doug Williams (grade 13), for misallocating funds from payroll. In addition, an African American division manager, Royce Watkins (grade 15), in Suburban was terminated by Clarence Thomas. The company did a great job in positioning POC managers to fire POC employees.

In February, I applied for a position as a customer service supervisor. Human Resources Representative Anna Ball (white female, director of human resources in 2017) interviewed me and I felt that the interview went very well. I did not get the position because I was told that I did not have enough customer service experience. They hired an external candidate Toni Boyd (African American female, grade 14). This was the 3rd position I applied for at the Sankofa Times and was not selected.

In May, I applied for a suburban division manager position. The suburban divisions were perceived as the "cream of the crop" for publications success. The suburban division manager position encompassed single copy (delivering newspapers to retailers) and home delivery (delivering newspapers to residential homes) operations. Its job scope was broader than city home delivery or single copy only divisions. To move up in the publication department it was a critical requirement to have single copy experience.

I was interviewed by regional managers Mary Cash (white female, grade 17), Clarence Thomas (African American, grade 17), and John Andy (white male, grade 17).

Mary was a smooth politician with great communication skills. She knew how to work the room and connect with senior management. Clarence was a dark-skinned black man who never challenged the status quo. He had a quiet demeanor and was viewed as "Safe."

My interview went very well with Mary Cash. My interview with John Andy was strange. He did not give me any eye contact throughout the entire 45-minute interview. My interview with Clarence went very well. He mentored me throughout the interview. Of course, I did not get the position. Jerry Trump (white male) who was already a division manager in Chicago city home delivery function, was selected for one of the open suburban divisions. Scott White (white male) was automatically promoted to Jerry's vacant division position with no internal posting to attract other qualified candidates.

In June at mid-year, my base salary was increased to $23,205 annually.

Table 2.0

The minimum for a grade 12 was $22,870. The midpoint was $30,494. The maximum was $38,117.

During my *first* annual review (August 2009), my performance was rated "above average." I received a

10% increase on my base salary, coupled with a promotion to field service account manager (grade 13). My new annual 2009 base salary was now $25,525.

Table 3.0

> The minimum for a grade 13 was
> $25,177. The midpoint was $33,570.
> The maximum was $41,962.

The company promotion increase guidelines recommended a 10 to 12% increase for promotions with a merit increase. As a field service member, there were three levels within the job's family: field service account coordinator (grade 12), field service account manager (grade 13), field service transition manager (grade 14).

In September, I applied for another division manager position in the city home delivery department. I was not selected. John Murk (white male) was promoted to the position.

Clarence Thomas was promoted from suburban regional manager to city street sales manager (grade 18). Eventually, Allen Baylor, an African American division manager (grade 15) in suburban, was also fired or pressured to leave.

In October, I applied for another division manager position, in the city street sales department. Clarence Thomas interviewed me and I felt that his interview style was very unprofessional. For the first time, I saw a different side of Clarence Thomas. During most of the interview, he stared at the ceiling. I even asked him; "Am I boring you?" Of course, I was not selected for the position.

Division manager, Terry Payton (African American male), was demoted and eventually he left the company. I applied for his open division manager position. Ron McDonald promoted Will Smith to the position. I felt that it was unfair that they promoted Will instead of myself. I had worked on most of the accounts in ex-Terry's south side division. I had more operations experience than Will. However, Will Smith was viewed as "safe" and smiled a lot.

In November, I applied for a division manager position in the national division. National manager Jane Libby (white female) interviewed me. She really did not interview me; she just talked *at* me during the entire interview. I did not get the position.

In December 2009, Ron McDonald invited me to breakfast and promoted me to division manager (grade 15). I received a 14% increase in my annual salary. My new grade 15 base salary was now $29,099 per year.

Table 4.0

The minimum for a job grade 15 was $34,244. The midpoint was $45,658. The maximum was $57,073.

I also received a promotion congratulation letter from Steve Gates, vice president and director of publications. I replaced June Smith in the South side of Chicago. June Smith was reassigned and became the first African American given an opportunity to manage the premier Gold-coast area in Chicago.

Out of 30+ employees formally recognized, I also received the 2009 Special Recognition award for outstanding performance in the publication department. In January 2010, I received a special congratulation letter from Mary Pelosii, director of customer satisfaction.

FY2009 CONCLUSIONS – LESSONS LEARNED:

- Corporate America: Good progress in promoting POCs to offset the losses of POCs. However, make sure that you're focusing on promoting POCs for the right reasons; they are the best qualified for the position. A risk in promotions is when you pay POCs at the bottom of the company's job scale. POCs will eventually notice this, and look outside the company for better pay equity. And, where is your mentoring program? As POCs start to move up the corporate ladder, this is the best time to assign them experienced company mentors.

- People of Color: In your second year of employment, to receive two promotions in a 12-month period is a great accomplishment. Continue to perform and be willing to accept challenges in your new role. You will now be under the corporate microscope.

YEAR 3
(2010)

IN 2010, RON McDonald created a new management position in the city home delivery function,
named city operations manager. He promoted division manager Mitt McToole (white male, grade 16)
to the position. Mitt did not have a college degree.
This position required a college degree or ten years
of equivalent work experience. He was short and
smoked a lot of cigarettes. He joked a lot and always kissed Ron's ass. I now reported directly to
Mitt.

In June, Mitt rated me "above average" for my six-
month performance review as a division manager.
I received a 17.7% increase in my annual salary

(to bring me to the minimum in a job grade 15 at $34,244). My new annual salary was now $34,250.

Table 5.0

> The minimum for a job grade 15 was $34,244. The midpoint was $45,658. The maximum was $57,073.

During the summer, June Smith and myself applied for a suburban division manager position. Regional Manager Jay Cutler (white male) interviewed both of us, but decided to promote Brad Grady (white male). Brad was a former management trainee who did not have the experience that June had in terms of managing a division. June eventually left the company as a disgruntled employee.

Earl was promoted to regional manager (grade 17) in suburban publications in October. His previous position, field training and development manager (grade 16) position was posted, so I applied for the position because of my past success in the department. Ron McDonald promoted division manager

Dick Young (white male with a college degree) to the position. I was told that I needed more publications experience. Now the city home delivery department, which was responsible for a predominately African American and Hispanic markets (53%) at the time, was being managed by three white managers. Later in the year, I was appointed as a key member for the company's minority promotions committee headed by Ron McDonald. The purpose of this committee was to provide consumer insights and revenue-generating programs in minority markets.

Incidentally, Jeff Sessions (white male) and Jane Wilkes (white female) were hired as management trainees for the 2010 publication management training program. I provided Jeff a personal overview and tour of my division when he visited the city home delivery area.

In 2010, I had a very good performance year. I improved service levels in 100% of my service categories. Also, I was the only POC manager selected to work on a special assignment in New York City, during the New York Star union strike. After my five-week special assignment in the Big Apple, I received thank you letters from Bill Gates (white male), Sankofa company president & CEO, John Murdock (white male), president and publisher of the Sankofa Company, and Steve Gates.

In December, I was rated "above average" by Mitt McToole. I received a 5.5% increase in my base salary. My annual salary was now $36,134 per year. Incidentally, Mr. "Safe", Will Smith was one of the 2010 Special Recognition Award winners.

FY2010 CONCLUSIONS – LESSONS LEARNED:

- Corporate America: Optics matter in a company. Make sure your leadership team is not 100% homogeneous or comprised of only white males. Employees will notice at all levels (senior, middle, first level) the mix of race and gender on your leadership team. And don't say you can't find or promote qualified POCs and women. Diversity brings the best ideas to the table.

- People of Color: It's a great decision to accept special assignments outside your standard duties. This is a great way to expand your brand across other departments and companies owned by your parent company. This is how you differentiate performance and receive senior leadership recognition.

YEAR 4
(2011)

IN 2011, AFTER several assignments in other functional areas, Publication Management Trainee Graduate Malcolm Jones (African American, grade 12) was promoted to division manager (grade 15) in the city home delivery function. For the first time in its history, the city home delivery function had three African American's out of seven divisions. Will Smith managed the downtown loop area, Malcolm (Southwest side) and myself (Southeast side) managed mainly African American and Hispanic markets.

In May, all three of us (including Mr. Safe, Will Smith) collectively identified a pattern of discrimination in our work environment. It was very clear to us that Mitt McToole and Ron McDonald treated White employees better than they treated us. It was a "good-ole-boy" network that did not include POCs. Ron and Mitt always verbally joked and called our minority divisions, "ghetto divisions" in staff meetings. This was racially offensive to us. Not all African Americans lived in ghettos.

We identified fourteen company practices that we found as inconsistent to the treatment of white managers.

Before we scheduled a meeting with Ron and Mitt to review our concerns, we decided to meet with the two highest ranked minority managers in the company for consultation. Will Smith selected EEO and Employment Manager Howard Clark (African American male, grade 17) from the human resources department. Malcolm selected Clarence Thomas (African American male, grade 17) from the publication department. When we met with Howard, he gave us very objective advice and he stated that he would support our endeavor. Later in the day, when we met with Clarence, he took a different approach and suggested that we "tone-down" our verbiage and use safer words such as "inconsistency" and not use "discrimination." After our meeting with Clarence, he immediately called his immediate white boss; Director of Publication's Hugh Heff (white male, grade 18). Clarence felt an obligation to warn senior management about our meeting. He broke our verbal agreement of confidentiality. We were very upset with Clarence Thomas.

In the next week, Ron McDonald called each one of us individually into his office. He became very irate and condescending when he met with each one of us. As a thin-skinned Irish hothead, Ron was always known for losing his temper and verbally abusing managers. We expressed to Ron that we wanted to meet with him as a group so that we could go over our fourteen issues. We met with Ron in May 2011 and expressed our beliefs of discriminatory practices in his function. There was a lot of tension in the room. Ron was very apprehensive and he even used the "nigger" word several times in our meeting, stating that by saying the "nigger" word does not mean that he is racist, and we should accept his leadership style.

Later, Hugh Heff met with me one-on-one to also go over these issues. He stated that I've been going on a good upward path in the company and he did not want me to veer of the path. Also, he stated that when we make statements as we did about white managers, that those statements could destroy a person with a family, i.e., Mitt McToole.

In June, Malcolm Jones submitted a request to Ron for the documented minutes from our May 2011 meeting. Ron met with Malcolm privately in a one-on-one and stated that he never made any notes of our meeting. Ron also verbally abused Malcolm for even inquiring about meeting notes. Later in the evening, Will Smith and Malcolm came to my home. Malcolm was very upset and crying because Ron had treated him so poorly. At that time, we all knew that Ron and Mitt were going to reassign us to different functions or terminate us for speaking up. Malcolm and myself shared the same office location.

In 2011, I had an outstanding performance year. Since my division market was more than 90% African American, I took advantage of my knowledge, relationships, and developed strategies to grow this unique market. I worked with Marcy (white female), Jim (white male) and Will Smith to re-establish our presence in the African American market. Due to my efforts, the Sankofa Times participated in the Chosen Few Picnic, Black Expo Chicago, Taste of Chicago, Puerto Rican fest, and Bud Billiken Day parade. These activities were the largest minority events in Chicago. Because of our efforts, Will Smith and myself received a personal thank you letter from two senior executives, Hugh Heff and Steve Gates.

In addition, I received a personal thank you letter from John Murdock, president & publisher, for being a Hire the Future mentor. I also received another thank you letter from John Murdock for being a solicitor for the Sankofa Times's 2011 Crusade of Mercy campaign. I was also selected to participate in a company-wide customer satisfaction strategy confirmed by a letter from John.

Later in the summer, Will Smith left the department and took a demotion (grade 13) to initiate a new career in the marketing department. I was re-assigned to a division in the North side of Chicago in which 1% of the market was minority. Malcolm remained at the South side office while I moved to the Wrigleville office. We all knew that our career with the Sankofa Times was now questionable. We felt that we would be scrutinized on the job every day. We did not trust the company's middle management team to provide an equal work environment for POCs.

Surprisingly, the two newly hired publication management trainees for the year were African American males; Joe Sargent (grade 12) and Hussein Canal (grade 12). Both men exemplified the perfect prototype of professional attributes that Clarence Thomas believed were necessary to move beyond the glass ceiling (grade 18 & above) in this company. Joe and Hussein were intelligent, college graduates, handsome, tall, articulate and true professionals.

In December, Mitt McToole rated my performance "exceptional" for my annual performance review. I received a 7% increase in my base salary. My new annual salary was now $38,663.

Table 6.0

> The minimum for a job grade
> 15 was $35,271. The midpoint
> was $45,658. The maximum was
> $58,785.

Also, I was selected as one of the department leaders for the company sponsored "Interpersonal Selling Strategies" course. Only the top performing division and field training and development managers were selected to facilitate this course, which included Lydia Pottman (white female - MBA from Northwestern University, now vice president at the Los Angeles Sentinel). I was the only POC selected to this program. We were charged with training 165 field publication managers on interpersonal selling strategies.

Furthermore, I received my second annual "Special Recognition" award for outstanding performance in 2011. I received congratulation letters from President John Murdock and Hellen Hope, vice president and director of human resources.

FY2011 CONCLUSIONS – LESSONS LEARNED:

- Corporate America: A claim of discrimination is a serious matter. Racial slurs and jokes should never be tolerated in a work environment. A zero-tolerance policy and anti-retaliation policy are best practices. Train and certify 100% of your people managers on an annual basis on how to effectively manage discrimination claims. Develop a 90-day action plan on corrective actions to prevent these claims in the future. Don't jump to legal defense. Jump to objective problem resolution by initiating an investigation. The investigation should not be based on gathering information to protect the company. The investigation should be based on targeting the root-cause issues and resolving them.

- People of Color: It is high risk career impacting decision to voice discrimination to company management or human resources. Remember, you did nothing wrong. Now is the time to over-perform and continue to prove that your value and talent is important for the company's long-term success. Stay focused and stay strong! Great companies value employees that speak up. If your company does not value an open and candid culture, then you may need to consider moving on to a better company.

YEAR 5
(2012)

I SENSED AT the beginning of 2012 that I would be re-assigned to a suburban division. In a one-on-one meeting I had with Clarence Thomas, he stated that I would never move up the management ranks if I continued to work on "black projects." He stated that I would eventually have to acquire single copy delivery experience in the suburban area and work in White markets before I would ever be given a higher position.

In January, Mitt McToole was promoted (grade 17) to a newly created position in the new alternate delivery department. He reported to Mary Cash (white female) who was promoted to director of alternate delivery (grade 18).

Mitt's position was posted and I applied for it. I felt that I had proven myself at this point in my career and that I had a good chance to succeed in this position. Ron McDonald selected field training and development manager Billie Bob (white male) as the new city home delivery operations manager. Billie had no experience in the city of Chicago and he did not have a college degree. Billie started in the company three months before I did.

In February, I applied for the 2012 Institute for Journalism Education Management Training Center, sponsored by the Maynard Institute. This was an eight-week management training program held at Northwestern University. The program was designed for diversity in the workforce for management. I was not selected for the position.

Later in the month Dick Young (white male) accepted a newly created position in the sales department. His position was posted. I applied for the field training and development manager (grade 16) position for the second time in my career. Ron McDonald promoted division manager Dave Duke (white male), to the position. Dave did not have a college degree. However, he had fifteen years of publication experience.

In April, I was transferred to a suburban publication division in the Montgomery County region. I did not receive any additional compensation even though my work load doubled. I was very apprehensive about this move. Every manager knew that Regional Manager Bill Casper (white male) was a nightmare to work for. He represented your true definition of an autocratic type manager. Tasks came first, people came last. My first three months were terrible. I was given one of the highest growing and most scrutinized publication markets in the company, encompassing Oak Brook, Naperville, Warrenville, Lisle, Downers Grove, and Wheaton.

I received no guidance or direction from him. He always made me feel absolutely inferior. I struggled trying to learn the single copy retail operations because of the pressure to excel. I had no experience working on single copy sales. The single copy operations accounted for 80% of a division manager's annual sales bonus in suburban publication.

Clarence Thomas warned me that the move was so that they could "watch" me. Earl Floyd told me that Bill was trying to get rid of me because he did not know how to manage a POC.

In June, I applied for a lower grade/demotion position in human resources. Bill Casper wrote in my letter of recommendation for the position: *"Norm has reported to me for less than 3 months. However, during this short time he has demonstrated a superior ability in the areas of agent operations and customer satisfaction. Norm's follow-through skills are exceptional and he is committed to achieving a high level of performance."*

I was not chosen for the senior employment specialist position. Division Manager Malcolm Jones also applied for the position. An external candidate, Judy Gill, was hired (African American female with no college degree) into the position.

The suburban publication functional manager, Tim Irish, was promoted to a higher position in another company. Ron McDonald was promoted to the suburban publication manager position (grade 18).

John Andy (white male) was promoted to city street sales manager (grade 18). Clarence Thomas was re-assigned to the city home delivery manager position (grade 17, lateral move). All three reported to Hugh Heff, director of publications.

In the middle of the summer, Bill was reassigned to manage the Lake region. He appointed me to "acting" regional manager until the Montgomery region was filled. I ran one of the most important regions for more than four weeks. In September, Angela Clark was promoted to regional manager (grade 17). This move was questioned by most of the managers because Angela's performance as field training and development manager was perceived as questionable. She did not have a good record of accomplishments and developing employees. She was docile and very loyal to the company. As an African American, if you were loyal and docile, you normally were perceived as "safe." Gary Knight (an openly gay white male), was more qualified and respected for the position.

Furthermore, I won the 2nd Quarter Directors award for the creation of a computerized trivia game used at Black Expo Chicago 2012. The game attracted overwhelming interest and positive consumer response at the Expo. As a result, Sankofa realized a 50% increase in number of sales leads over the previous year. This promotional program was utilized to further strengthen the Sankofa Times's presence within POC communities.

I also performed very well in my White dominated suburban division. For the first time under my leadership, we participated in the Naperville Ribfest, Irish Parade, Nights of Italy, GermanFest, and the Naperville Business Expo. I received positive performance feedback from senior management.

Incidentally, one of the 2012 publication management trainees hired was an African American female, Tiffani Hill.

The field training and development (grade 16) position vacated by Angela Clark was now posted. For the third time in my career, I applied for the position. Ron McDonald promoted Division Manager Alex Cortez (Hispanic, grade 16) into the position. I was shocked and deeply disappointed by Ron's decision. I was the most qualified for the position and I was disregarded. Alex was another docile and loyal manager. He had no backbone and no record of achievement. He was "Safe."

In December, I was rated "exceptional" by new regional manager, Angela Clark, for my annual performance review. I received a 5.6% increase in my annual salary. My base salary was now $40,828.

Table 7.0

The minimum for a job grade 15 was $37,799. The midpoint was $49,700. The maximum was $61,600.

The company "merit increase guidelines" recommend a 7 to 8% increase for current salaries that are below the midpoint.

She also nominated me for the 2012 President Award, the department's highest honor and the 4th Quarter Director's Award. Division Manager Jerry Trump (white male) won the President's award, and then left the company to become a delivery agent. Division Manager Malcolm Jones (African American) was one of the 2012 Special Recognition Award winners.

FY2012 CONCLUSIONS – LESSONS LEARNED:

- Corporate America: Reassigning and promoting POCs should be based on their performance and past accomplishments. Employees will notice when you promote "Token" or "Safe" POCs for the wrong reasons. White males are normally promoted based on potential, not performance. When you don't promote POCs because of proven performance, they will eventually fail and leave the company.

- People of Color: Okay, you've finally been assigned to a highly visible role and premier market. Take advantage of your new assignment and "hit it out of the park." Overdeliver and demonstrate that you can learn the business, you are adaptable, you build relationships, and are able to effectively grow predominantly White markets and business accounts. This is a great opportunity to show senior management your value proposition.

YEAR 6
(2013)

THE YEAR 2013 was my worst year ever at the Sankofa Times. Working for an African American manager, Angela Clark, was a nightmare. She was incompetent, disorganized, lazy, power-oriented and threatened by my confidence and knowledge of the job. We basically disagreed on everything.

She only managed by power, not by relationships. I felt that she was trying to get rid of me. She always supported white independent delivery agents before she would support her own minority employees. I knew that she was building a file on my performance. My consumption of alcohol escalated and I became an alcoholic in January. I did meet with

Jenny Grambly from human resources to discuss the stress level from the job and its environment.

My objective was to get away from Angela Clark. I sensed that the company was trying to get rid of me (POC) through her (POC). I did not feel any job security.

In February 2013, I received my five-years of service pin from Ron McDonald. Also, I applied for the 2013 Institute for Journalism's Management Training Center for the 2nd time in a year. I was not selected. Ron McDonald was selected for this minority leadership program.

In March 2013, I applied for the field training and development manager (grade 16) position for the fourth time in my career. City home delivery manager, Clarence Thomas promoted Division Manager Jerry Gately (white male) to the position. Clarence told me that Jerry was a safer move for him. He stated that senior management would question his decision to promote me. However, he stated that management would not question his decision to promote a white male.

In June 2013, I was surprised that Angela Clark nominated me for the 2nd Quarter Director Award for Sales Excellence. Out of 45 managers, I won the Award.

In July 2013, I was unhappy, depressed, and demotivated, so I applied for an operations analyst position in the operations department. I knew that Angela would support my decision to become an analyst. However, I did not get the position. I never received any feedback on who received the position.

In August 2013, I applied for the national transition and transportation position (grade 16) in national publications. I interviewed with Mary Cash (white), then the director of national publication. The interview went very well. She promoted Division Manager John McCain (white male) to the position.

In September 2013, the suburban publication department was realigned to match our editorial zoned editions. Angela Clark was reassigned to a smaller publication region, the Gary region.

Regional manager Jay Cutler (white male) was assigned to the Montgomery region, the largest publication region in the company. Jay was 6'7", weighed over 300 pounds, and never smiled. He was super smart, analytical, and well-respected by senior management. I now reported directly to Jay.

In addition, I volunteered to participate in a first ever, company-wide diversity roundtable for POCs with the new Sankofa Times President and CEO Jerry Jones (white male). The session gave me hope, because I realized that there were a lot of POCs who felt the same way that I did about the company. We all expressed to Jerry Jones that management practices were discriminatory. Of course, Jerry stated that they were working on it.

In October 2013, I applied for the field training and development manager (grade 16) position for the fifth time. City Home Delivery Manager Clarence Thomas promoted Division Manager Moochie Relf (African American female) to the position. Clarence told me that Moochie had been employed in the company longer and that she was "Safe." He suggested that I needed to work more on being a political champion like Joe Sargent (one of Clarence's favorite African Americans). My direct manager, Jay Cutler (white male), felt that Clarence's promotion decision was poor because Moochie has never delivered any major results in her 15-year tenure.

In December, I was rated "above average" for my annual performance review. I received a 3.5% increase in my annual salary. My salary was now $42,258.

Table 8.0

The minimum for a job grade 15 was $38,933. The midpoint was $50,800. The maximum was $63,448.

The company recommended merit increase guidelines is a 4 to 6% increase for salaries below the midpoint.

Jay stated that my previous manager, Angela Clark, provided the most input on my review. I told him that I had disagreed with the rating because I had my best performance year as a division manager.

Jay stated, "It's not my fault that you worked for a God-awful manager." Incidentally, Joe Sargent (African American) was one of the 2013 Special Recognition Award winners.

FY2013 CONCLUSIONS – LESSONS LEARNED:

- Corporate America: Kudos to the new CEO for hosting a diversity roundtable. This is a bold first step to build inclusion in your company. Also, include white employees in the roundtable discussions, as their input and feedback are just as important. The biggest challenge a company will experience is how do you cascade these expectations on Diversity and Inclusion (D&I) throughout middle management. Middle management and 1st-level supervisors are your biggest barriers and naysayers. Require mandatory D&I training for all people managers and tie in their hiring, promotion and retention targets to their annual goals and bonus.

- People of Color: The good news, you now have a new manager: white male. Move forward and focus on the future. You did not receive a promotion, which is okay. Build a strong relationship with your new manager and prove to him/her why you are one of his best employees in the company. It's time to roll up your sleeves, dig deep, and demonstrate your natural value.

YEAR 7
(2014)

THE COMPANY'S PERFORMANCE rating scale was amended in FY2014, reflecting: 2=Needs Improvement, 3=Achieves Standards, 4=Exceeds Standards, 5=Exceptional.

In January, I applied for the Sankofa Leadership Development Program (LDP) in the operations department. This was a program designed to increase diversity in the operations department. I interviewed with Jim O'Reilly (white male, grade 20), the vice president of operations. I also went through a panel interview with all of Jim's seven direct reports. The entire panel was 100% white males. This was also the first time that I met with Director Rudy Doyle (white male, grade 18).

Jay Cutler wrote in my letter of recommendation for the position: *"Norm is very strong operationally in Publications. He is very Goal oriented and pushed himself to perform above his peers. Norm has exceptional follow-up and written and analytical skills. I believe that Norm has tremendous potential to continue developing as a manager. At this point he is certainly ready for additional responsibility within the company."*

A white female, already a director in operations was chosen for the position.

Jay was the first manager outside of Earl Floyd to empower me. He was very supportive of my decisions and respected my knowledge of the business. As a white male, Jay was an aberration. I believe that he was more open to POCs because of his experience working with African Americans as a blue-chip college football player at Alabama University.

He was also the first manager to showcase my public communication skills at one of our monthly senior management customer satisfaction meetings. For the first time in my career, I presented the 7th Period service results to the senior management team.

After the presentation, I received rave reviews from Steve Gates (white male), the director of metro publication, Britt Johnson (white male), the director of national publication, Mary Cash (white female), and the director of planning & analysis, Tom Brady (white male).

With Jay's support, I gave him 110% effort on all my assignments and projects. I built a very strong relationship with all of my independent contractors.

In December, I was rated "exceptional" for my annual performance review. I received a 4.75% increase in my annual salary. My salary was now $44,265.

Table 9.0

> The minimum for a job grade 15 was $40,101. The midpoint was $52,324. The maximum was $65,351.

The company recommended merit increase guidelines recommended a 7 to 8% increase for current salaries below the midpoint.

Jay also nominated me for the 2014 President's Award.

FY2014 CONCLUSIONS – LESSONS LEARNED:

- Corporate America: Recognize white managers that are effective in managing POCs. Terminate white managers that have a track record of losing POC talent. Your company will be more profitable when you embrace diversity & inclusion and reward the leadership behaviors that strengthen your diverse talent pool. As any Fortune 500 board will tell you, diversity wins in today's market.

- People of Color: Good job! It's critical in your career to demonstrate that you can work for white managers and excel. You and your new manager are now role models on what good working relationships look like. Continue to perform at a high-level and always thank your new manager for being so supportive. The more "positive" White relationships you build, the better for you in the long-term. Your manager can be a professional reference for life.

YEAR 8
(2015)

IN JANUARY 2015, I was reassigned to my fourth publication division. Back in November 2014, I was told by Jay Cutler and Ron McDonald that I would be working on the LakeSide strategy. This was the most important strategic priority for the Sankofa Times Company. Unfortunately, the regional manager at the time was Angela Clark. However, the other division managers believed that Angela was going to be transferred from the LakeSide region. They felt that she would not be able to handle the company's number one revenue growth initiative, the LakeSide strategy.

Rudy Doyle (white male), the director of production, was appointed to the position of director, metro publication. Britt Johnson left the company for a higher position at the Los Angeles News in California.

In February, I was awarded the 2014 President's Award. The President Award is the department's highest honor for truly outstanding achievement. It is for job performance which places the individual in a special class of dedication, commitment, and accomplishment. The individual must meet the finest tradition of the department and embody the values for which the Sankofa Times stands. At this milestone in my career, I knew that I would finally "Break" the glass ceiling: Professional grade 18 and above. My name was now listed in the Department's Hall of Fame.

On February 20th, Billie Bob (white, no degree, grade 17 - promoted to regional manager in October 2013), regional manager for the DeKalb Region, was transferred to the LakeSide region.

During this month, I applied for the home delivery manager position at the Sankofa Company's sister publication in Miami, Florida, the Miami Times. Incidentally, Hugh Heff (white male, promoted from Sankofa to the Miami Times) was the new vice president of publication at the Miami Times. I was only given a phone interview by the hiring manager. I found out eight weeks later that they hired a white male from another company.

Later on in the year, I realized that I was not transferred to work on the LakeSide strategy, renamed the McDonald edition. Billie Bob only required me to work during the McDonald edition launch by delivering a sample paper route for one week. The implementation plan was developed by division manager's Tommy Boy (white male - no college degree), Billie Bob (white male - no college degree) and Bill Casper (white male - no college degree); who was promoted to suburban development operations manager (grade 18) in 2014. At 1:30 am as I was stuffing my paper route, I realized that Ron McDonald lied to me about this opportunity.

In May, I applied for the city home delivery operations and development manager position (grade 16). After five and half years as a successful division manager, I knew that I was the most qualified candidate for this position.

Home Delivery Manager Clarence Thomas selected Jared Trump (white male with an MBA). After only one year in the company, Jared was promoted ahead of me. Clarence told me that Jared was high level and he had an MBA and experience working with budgets. Clarence knew that division managers were not given access to financial budgets. The only way you could acquire budget experience was being promoted to a grade 16 position.

In July, John McCain (white male) was promoted to regional sales manager (grade 17) in the suburban publication department. John McCain started his career two years after me. I trained him as a manager trainee in 2010.

I did not apply for the position. I felt that if I was not selected for a grade 16 position, then I had a lesser chance of being promoted to a grade 17 position.

At the end of the month, Rudy Doyle reorganized the publication management team structure. Rudy had all the characteristics of a great executive. He had his MBA and exceptional vision.

Ron McDonald was named to a new position (logistical planning) with no direct reports. Bill Casper was named to a position (distribution sales network) with no direct reports. John Andy's position was eliminated. Clarence Thomas was promoted to the director of national publication (grade 18). Mary Cash (white female) was named the director of metro publication south. Mitch Romney (white male) was named to director of metro publication north. A new position was created: director of distribution network development, later named to Jimmy Johns (white male). These changes made it very clear that Rudy wanted a "new" way of thinking from management. Everybody perceived the moves as the transformation from "old" school to "new" school. A move from non-college educated managers to MBA-educated leaders.

I now knew, in order to move up the leadership ranks, a college degree with work experience would not be good enough. I needed to pursue my MBA. I was accepted and enrolled part-time at DeVry University, Keller Graduate School of Management.

There were no POCs promoted. However, Clarence Thomas continued to flourish in the department. Earl Floyd and Angela Clark remained as the two "token" regional managers (grade 17).

In August, Clarence Thomas promoted Charnies Clark-Ryan to national sales operations manager (grade 16). Charnies was one of Clarence's favorite female proteges. Clarence felt that it was easier to promote an African American female than an African American male. He stated to me that senior management was afraid of African American males and did not feel comfortable around African American males. He stated to me that they (white management) would never give me the corporate *key* (promotion above the ceiling) to the corporate castle unless I was more like them.

In August, Customer Service Manager Stacy Banks (African American female) was promoted to publication consumer services director (grade 18) reporting directly to VP of Publications, Steve Gates.

Division Manager Malcolm Jones and myself became frustrated because of the lack of opportunities for African American males to move past a grade 15 position. Will Smith was still at a grade 14 level *in* marketing. He saw the same level of discrimination in marketing.

We were going to send the following letter to Mr. Jerry Jones, but Malcolm requested that I hold on to the letter until we see more changes from Rudy Doyle. We assumed that Rudy would create more opportunities for African Americans:

Letter Drafted in August 2015

August 2015

To: Jerry Jones

President and Publisher

Re: *THE AFRICAN-AMERICAN MALE*

Dear Mr. Jones:

We represent a group of African American "males" and Sankofa Times full-time employees who are frustrated, disgruntled and embarrassed over the past and current practices of the publication times management team. It is very clear and obvious that the African American male is either feared or forgotten when the time comes to reach or surpass the professional grade level 18 (technically our glass ceiling at the director-level). Each one of us has been employed with the Sankofa Times for more than five years. We are also college graduates and aspire to pursue our MBA.

First and foremost, we do not play basketball, we are not in a gang, we are not on welfare, we do not listen to rap music, we do not live in public housing and we believe in personal hygiene. Now that the preconceived notions are eliminated, please review and fathom the following thoroughly analyzed facts.

FACT #1: SEASONED VETERANS

The Sankofa Times is the flagship of Sankofa Company, one of the top media corporations in the country. The newspaper has been published continuously since December 1, 1917. In its 100 years of history, only four African American males have reached or surpassed the ambiguous "Grade level 17 (or 16)," in our department. The pioneers are; Mr. Anthony Herron, a 13-year veteran, Mr. Clarence Thomas, an 18-year veteran, Mr. Earl Floyd, a 20-year veteran, and Mr. Alberto Alford, a 6-year veteran who left the company in 2007 for a better offer from a smaller newspaper. Three AA males have reached this marquee level in the 2000s, and ONLY one has reached it in the 2010s.

The three veterans who are still in our department, have been programmed to forget that they are still African American men. They have forgotten that true diversity begins with differences in vision, innovation, culture, heritage and history. They could never be true mentors to young aspiring African American male employees, because they still condone "old school political practices."

They have mastered the skill to not diplomatically challenge or question any inconsistencies in our developmental practices and promotional decisions.

Incidentally, they are all very deserving of their positions and accomplishments, since two of them began their careers as Sankofa "truck drivers."

FACT #2: FEMALE, MORE PROMOTABLE

The African American female is perceived as less threatening when it comes to inheriting or acquiring different managerial positions within our team. In the past seven years, twenty-four African American females have occupied or are currently within grade levels 12 to 15. In the past seven years, twenty-four African American males have occupied or are currently within grade levels 12 to 15. In the past five years, two African American females have reached level 16, one has reached grade level 17, and one has reached level 18. Apart from Anthony, Earl and Clarence, apparently there are no qualified African American males in our department, because none have been promoted to grade 16 and above. The four females are also pioneers who have broken the glass ceiling.

FACT #3: COLLEGE DEGREE, YES/NO

In the past five years, seven white males were promoted to level 16 and above with NO college degree. In the same span, not one African American male was promoted to level 14 and above, without a college degree. There are 37 positions that fall within grade levels 16 and 21. Again, only our three veteran males hold positions within this group. Whatever happened to "new school" or "new leadership" or "new vision?" Only one African American male was promoted to grade 17 or above in the 2010s; and we call ourselves building a strategic awareness and preparing for the information superhighway of the 21st century.

FACT #3: MANAGERS ON THE FAST TRACK

The department identifies high potential employees with and without degrees and places them on a "fast track." Over the past five years, there have been six white males that have reached or surpassed the professional grade level of a "16." The question remains, how did they get there? Were these managers high performers, did they walk the walk and talk the talk, were they led along the way, were they given a chance to prove themselves, or did the hiring manager feel comfortable with someone that represented their same kinship? If that is the case, who will embrace the true meaning of diversity and inclusion for the African American male?

There have been twelve African American males in this department who reached the same level as their white colleagues at grade 15. The question remains, why aren't we promotable after that point? Do we become stagnant at that point because we know who we are and whose we are. Are we perceived as individuals who will question and propose change when inconsistencies are discovered, or is it merely the fact that we are African American males?

CONCLUSION

We should not promote African American males because they are programmed. We should promote and develop African American males because; 1. They adhere to the Sankofa Company's values. 2. They have great potential as future leaders. 3. They have excelled in their current and past jobs. 4. They have past and proven professional accomplishments. 5. They are scrupulous human beings with high integrity. 6. They embody and honor our company's mission. 7. They continue to build their knowledge and education and are role models in the company.

End of letter

———◦◦◦———

In October, Jay Cutler was promoted to director of planning & analysis (grade 18) in the publication operations department. His previous position as regional manager for the Montgomery County region was posted. Billie Bob was transferred to Jay's region and became my immediate supervisor. Billie was a soft manager with no backbone. In private, he told another white manager that he was happy that blacks did not attend the company's annual golf outing.

I applied for the open region Billie vacated. I felt very good about my chances since I'd mastered the suburban publication operations. Metro Publication South Director Mary Cash promoted Jeff Sessions (white male) to a grade 17. Jeff was currently a grade 15. It was an aberration to promote a grade 15 employee two levels to a grade 17 position. However, everybody in management knew that Rudy Doyle loved Jeff Sessions. He was viewed as the golden white Irish boy that walked on water.

Mary stated to me that I did a great job in the interview and to hang in there; something good would eventually happen to me.

In November, I was invited by VP Steve Gates to participate in my second diversity roundtable discussion. White males, white females, and POCs attended this discussion. The most common complaints that were expressed to Steve was the "lack of movement and promotions for POCs" and "the good-ole-boy network" brick wall. The good news, the white males also agreed to the concerns. Steve stated that senior management would address our concerns.

In December, based on majority input from Jay Cutler, Billie Bob rated my performance "exceptional" for my annual performance review. I received a 5% increase in my annual salary. My new base salary was $46,478.

Table 10.0

> The minimum for a job grade 15 was $41,600. The midpoint was $53,300. The maximum was $67,312.

Billie Bob nominated Tommy Boy (white male) for the President's Award. I was very upset that he did not nominate me after I had another stellar year under adverse conditions. Billie never provided me any "feedback" on my skills or areas that I needed to improve on for the entire year. Billie and Tommy used to go out weekly on "one-on-one" lunches together. In the past twelve months, Billie never invited me to a "one-on-one" lunch with him.

Letter I sent to Billie Bob.

December 2015

Mr. Billie A. Bob, Regional Manager

3800 S. Lincoln Road, Chicago Heights, IL

Mr. Bob:

In order to build our association for 2016, I wanted to provide you with a synopsis on my accomplishments in 2015.

I was informed on November 30, 2014, that I would be reassigned to the LakeSide region to support the McDonald edition strategy by contributing my expertise in publication. At first, I was a little leery, because I was leaving an exciting "high growth" division in the Montgomery county region which I felt was just as strategically important as McDonald county. Consequently, I decided to accept my reassignment and objectively approached the LakeSide strategy as a great opportunity to apply my skills and talent.

On January 2015, I officially became responsible for division #911. I was able to identify the fact that there was no growth potential in my new area. Division #911 was definitely a "low maintenance" area in terms of Sankofa readership. As far as my involvement in the McDonald strategy, it only amounted to my role in delivering a 150 paper sample route at 1:00 am at our Gurnee facility from April 10th through April 14th.

Since I was not given the opportunity to sparkle in a strategically important, company supported initiative; 2015 was still a great year. Therefore, that is why I propose that all "Rewards and Recognition" programs be based on the employee's ability to support the eight Sankofa Values.

If employees won awards (President's Award, Special Recognition, Director's Award) based on their contribution to our values, then we would probably eliminate all *political* inequities in our selection process. No employee can question our eight VALUES. Not every employee is given an opportunity to shine, but the best employees shine by their own merit. The eight values represent the bible that guides our thoughts and navigates our direction.

INTEGRITY: Integrity is the foundation of all we do. We hold ourselves to high standards of honesty, objectivity, independence and ethical conduct.

Example: 1 was challenged in 2015 with a unique and sometimes apathetic group of independent contractors. I demonstrated integrity by promoting the importance of honesty in the relationship between contractors and the Sankofa representative. Performance in all facets of our operations improved year over year and agents voluntarily reduced auto mileage expense by more than 1,000 miles per week, saving our company money in fixed costs.

CITIZENSHIP: Our businesses are leaders in their communities, and we encourage employee involvement in civic and charitable activities.

Example: In 2015, I volunteered my Saturdays to mentor young African American foster children for the Catholic Charities. Also, I spent time facilitating high school youth seminars for the 2015-2016 Alpha Lite Education Program. In 2016, I have volunteered to work as a teacher for the Junior Achievement Whole School Program.

CUSTOMER SATISFACTION: We anticipate the needs of our customers and strive to exceed their expectations. We build lasting and rewarding relationships through our responsiveness, efficiency, quality and ability to add value.

Example: Daily complaints were reduced by 14% year over year. Sunday complaints were reduced by 15% year over year. Multiple complaints were reduced by 24% year over year. Consequently, 2,236 additional customers were satisfied with our home delivery service in 2015. Historically, this is the best service year in this division.

INNOVATION: We value creativity, entrepreneurship and intelligent risk-taking.

Example: In April 2015, I submitted a proposal on the Internet. I felt that on-line resources represents the future. I have not received any feedback on the status of my proposal except that it was excellent. Also, I wrote a proposal on the need for modern Laptop computers at the end of 2014.

DIVERSITY: We value differences in ideas, people and cultures and strive to reflect these differences in our products and services.

Example: I volunteered for the Good Eating promotion, McDonald sampling program, Black Expo Chicago, Pilson YMCA auction and the Bud Billiken Parade, because I think that it is so important that our readers realize that the Sankofa Times represent a multi-cultural workforce. I represent diversity because of my differences in my opinions and my respect for all people. Our race is Sankofa red, white and blue.

FINANCIAL STRENGTH: We are committed to maximizing shareholder value over the long term. Strong financial resources enable us to reward our shareholders and employee owners, serve our customers, attract and develop the best people, and contribute to the vitality of our local communities.

Example: In 2015, I reduced outstanding money owed to the publisher by an average of $21,000 per week. When I started in the division, single copy outlets owed us 560 days in arrears. Today, that deficit has been reduced to only 56 days. Also, I utilized only 4% of the samples that the other

divisions distributed in the LakeSide region, thus reducing our exposure to additional costs in newsprint waste. Even though I lost 3% of the sales volume to the new McDonald launch, after three quarters, my division is 115% over goal in sales. In November, I eliminated the sports final edition at our Skokie facility, creating minimal impact to our Saturday readers and reducing operating costs for our transportation department.

TEAMWORK and EMPLOYEE INVOLVEMENT: Our success depends on our people. We work together toward common goals, exchange ideas and share resources. This same spirit of partnership is the key to long-term relationships with our customers and suppliers.

Example: In 2015, a team member of the agent retention committee, DC material handling committee, voice committee, single copy squad committee, standardization of paperwork task force, diversity committee, agent fees task force, division manager sales contest committee and the realignment of resources task force.

Current projects pending 2015/2016: 1) Alpha realignment project, 2) O'Hare Hotel expansion program, 3) Distribution center capacity analysis - metro north, 4) I recently applied for the technology assessment group.

MY BEST ACCOMPLISHMENT in 2015: The publication gap has been closed to the lowest margin in 10+ years. The division is down 96 (-0.3%) copies daily and 1,070 (-2%) copies on Sunday compared to 2014. In 2014, the division was down 1,058 (-4%) copies daily and 2,311 (-4%) copies on Sunday compared to 2013. In 2013, the division was down 1,535 (-5%) copies daily and 1,736 (-3%) copies on Sunday compared to 2012.

If you would like to discuss further, please let me know.

Sincerely,

Norman P. Fleming, Division Manager

Source: Special Report, Times Values, November 2015

———◆———

FY2015 CONCLUSIONS – LESSONS LEARNED:

• Corporate America: In a company sponsored diversity roundtable meeting, it is important to communicate the actions the company plans to take to improve diversity and inclusion. If employees take the risk to provide you candid feedback, then you should always follow-up with next steps and action plans. Any company in business should have diversity & inclusion goals and performance targets. Unfortunately, the white male homogeneous culture still dominates most corporate cultures today. Incidentally, Asian males

from the country of India are making progress in breaking the glass ceiling.

- People of Color: Continue to document
  your performance and make sure your new
  manager is aligned on your annual SMART
  (Specific, Measurable, Actionable, Realistic,
  Timebound) goals. Request feedback on your
  performance on a monthly basis. You don't
  want to be surprised in your year-end performance review. Also, if your manager does
  not invite you out for a one-on-one lunch,
  then you should take the lead and invite him/
  her out to lunch! In addition, get your MBA!
  Corporate America has raised the bar on
  minimum required (Bachelor) or preferred
  (Masters) education on a job application. As
  a POC you will not receive the benefit of the
  doubt when it comes to education or equivalent work experience.

YEAR 9
(2016)

IN JANUARY 2016, Mitch Romney (white male) and Mary Cash (white female) invited me to lunch and informed me that out of 50-plus candidates, that I was selected to manage the "field service team project." They stated that since I was a high potential (HiPo) with knowledge and vision, and that I was the perfect candidate to work on five goals to re-organize the field service team. Actually, I was temporarily replacing Alex Cortez as the field training and development manager (grade 16), since the position was going to be eliminated. Mitch and Mary both stated that they did not want to promote me into a position that was going to be eliminated. I was to report directly to Mary. Mitch Romney appointed himself to be my professional mentor for the year.

I officially took over the south field service team in Harvey, Illinois on January 29th. Alex was assigned to an analyst position working for Jay Cutler. Alex left the team in a total mess. Morale was low, the employees were not developed, their attitude was poor, and there was no infrastructure built for the field service operations. Alex did not do the job that he held for more than three years and he was given a lateral position.

I had to reengineer the entire operations and developmental program for six employees; George Shrimp (white male), Mike Woody (white male), Rosemary Tell (white female), Lorette McMoore (white female), Shawn Mack (white male), and Lebron Harris (African American, a former NFL football star).

I made an immediate impact and Mary noticed my stellar performance. She stated that she wanted to pay me for the good work that I was doing so she officially promoted me on February 29th.

After six consecutive years as a division manager (grade 15), I was finally promoted to field training and development manager, a professional grade 16 position. I received a 6% increase in my annual base salary. My new base salary was $49,268.

Table 11.0

The minimum for a job grade 16 was $48,300. The midpoint was $61,900. The maximum was $75,500.

Incidentally, she did remind me that my position would be eliminated in June 2016.

In March, Field Service Account Manager Lebron Harris was suspended and then fired after I investigated allegations brought to my attention by Field Service Account coordinator Lorette McMoore (white female). Lorette knew that Lebron was misallocating funds for personal use from Sankofa's payroll since October of 2015. However, she never brought it to management's attention until now.

In April, Mary authorized me to fire Lebron Harris for breaching several company policies. However, Mary did not approve me to provide Lorette

McMoore a verbal or written warning for withholding information about this situation. The company policy states, "Employees who suspect fraud have a responsibility to report it immediately to their supervisor or company legal counsel."

Furthermore, during Sankofa Company's corporate audit of the Harvey orientation account, I verified that Alex Cortez had approved payment of fees to an independent driver (Gary Truman) who did not work for three weeks. This was a violation of our company policy. When I informed Mary of my findings, she stated to me that she did not want to hear anything about Alex.

In addition, Mary did not support me on my documentation of Mike Woody's (white male) poor performance. She did not show the same sense of urgency that she displayed on the Lebron Harris case. She felt that I was picking on Mike Woody.

At the end of the month, the city field service team was eliminated and six employees were assigned to my team. I received mainly African American employees that worked for Jared Trump (white male).

Four POCs and two white males were assigned to me. Mike Woody, Rosemary Tell were re-assigned to the north suburban team managed by Pat Safe (white male).

The field service members I received from Jared's area had low morale, no developmental plans, and no sense of being valued by the organization. They all told me that Jared managed them by voice mail or e-mail. Division Manager Tom Long (white male) worked for Jared and stated to me in a private one-on-one that Jared did nothing for them.

Again, I re-engineered my field service operations because the five employees had no single copy experience. My objective was to train and develop them before my area was eliminated.

In April, Sankofa Times President and Publisher Jerry Jones announced major organizational changes for the Sankofa Times company. The creation of a

new department merged the publications with operations as a single division. Jim O'Reilly was named
vice president and director of the new department.
Jim was a short guy, around 5'4". He had a zero track
record in promoting POCs and seemed to feel un-
comfortable around them. I met him at a meeting in
New Orleans and it was a struggle for me to establish
any small talk with him. He did not even comment
on sports, which is normally an easy topic to discuss.

Steve Gates (white male) continued as vice president,
reporting to Jerry Jones. This was the company's
first ever major reorganization. The reorganization
created many new positions. However, Clarence
Thomas, Stacy Banks, Jesse Jackson (a 2-year employee who was in charge of the African American
sales strategy) were the only African Americans that
held key senior management positions.

In June, for the first time in my career, I participated
in the 2017 annual salary planning meeting for division managers (fifteen total employees). Division
managers Nancy Maza (Hispanic female), Phyliss

White (African American female), Howard Bean (white male), Malcolm Jones, Don Dummy (white male) were forecasted as being rated "needs improvement" in 2017, based on their current performance. The five division managers that were placed in the Exceptional, category were all white males.

Incidentally, Mike Woody was rated as "needs improvement" for 2017, by John McCain (white male) and Pat Right (white male). John called Mike Woody a "scumbag" in the meeting.

In July, Mary Cash (white female), Mitch Romney (white male), and Jimmy Johns (white male) announced the maximizing our talent reorganization in the distribution area of publications. A new middle level management team was formed. The team reflected: Jared Trump (white male), was promoted to regional manager (grade 17), Tom Suger (white male) was promoted to the new position of single copy sales and marketing manager (grade 17), Dave Duke (white male) was promoted to the new position of single copy operations manager (grade 18).

I was named to a lateral position, field technology manager (same grade 16 - no salary increase).

I was the only middle manager not promoted to a newly created position. Earl Floyd, Billie Bob, Jeff Sessions, John McCain, and Angela Clark remained as regional managers (grade 17).

The promotion of Jared Trump was a surprise to me. Jared's greatest deficiency was his interpersonal skills. Jared was very condescending and had consistently alienated other employees. He was just weird.

Incidentally, Earl (African American male) was assigned two "needs improvement" division managers; Don Dummy and Nancy Maza. Angela Clark (African American female) was assigned three "needs improvement" division managers; Phyliss White, Howard Bean, and Malcolm Jones. Incidentally, all three of her division managers left the company by the end of the year. My good friend, Malcolm was terminated by Angela because of poor performance. He received a separation package with eight weeks of salary.

Regional Manager Jeff Sessions (white male) received two "exceptional" rated division managers.

John McCain (white male) also received two "exceptional" division managers. Each regional manager was responsible for three division managers. It was very clear that Earl and Angela were not given talented human resources to succeed in their roles.

Tom Suger (white male) was assigned three direct reports and I was only given two direct reports. Later in the year, I was given my third direct report.

I implemented the field service reorganization plan on August 2016, while learning my new position. I actually did both jobs for five weeks. I was told that I would be responsible for supporting and managing all distribution/single copy related technology. I was given three publication division managers who had no previous experience or formal education or training in information technology. It was a struggle trying to grow this newly created functional area, because I had a group of employees with no experience. We all started in our new roles from ground zero. Furthermore, I was never given full responsibility of distribution/single copy related technology.

Dave Duke (white male) was still working with the single copy technology initiatives. Later on, Jennifer Macy (white female) took over the planning, Pete Oracle (white male) was responsible for our distribution systems and remoteware enhancements, Barb Boston (white female) and Diane Bany (white female) were responsible for scheduling employee computer training classes. John Corn (white male) was responsible for paging, mapping and multiple publications system enhancements. My involvement in technology was very vague, unstructured, and limited. With the assistance of Pete Oracle, I developed my own job description, my direct reports job descriptions, and annual technology training plan.

Systems and Technology Supervisor Steve Pace (white male) told me that I was placed in a "trick bag." He stated that I was put into a position to fail. He could not believe that I was given three employees with no systems or technology experience. Steve had fifteen years of information technology experience and he managed employees in the systems and technology department. System's Project Coordinator Rick Love also echoed the same feedback to me as Steve. Rick also had fifteen years of systems experience.

Furthermore, I received my "six" month performance (four months late) review from Mary in November 2016. Overall, it was positive, and I expected an "exceptional" rating for my annual review. It was informal and she did not provide me a rating. I still felt that I was not getting proper support from her to be successful in my new position.

In December, Mary, Mitch, and Jimmy Johns e-mailed the department's annual scorecard for 2016. This list of accomplishments was sent to the "matrix" management team [director level]. After reviewing the document, I noticed that Mary did not mention my involvement in one of the company's major projects.

The list reflected: Jeff Sessions – Montgomery market team, Jared Trump - niche publications, Mary Cash - ink on paper, Billie Bob, Jennifer Macy, Mary Cash - integrated manufacturing & distribution, Jared Trump - SW market segment team, John McCain - entertainment segment team, Bob Smith

- NSA project, Tom Suger - minority markets development team.

No POCs were mentioned under the "key company accomplishments" category. My name should have been included under the integrated publications project. I developed the "scope of the market" plan, in which the company invested $65,000 in consultants to assess. The market potential represented $76.5 million in incremental revenue from my plan.

FY2016 CONCLUSIONS – LESSONS LEARNED:

- Corporate America: It's always a best practice to create company approved job descriptions and pay grades before you announce a reorganization. No employee should ever be moved into a newly created role without a job description and potential salary increase or change. Also, monitor the assignments of employees in restructuring plans to ensure equity. Poor performing employees should not be assigned to only POC managers. There should be a balance and fairness in employee assignments.

- People of Color: If you are not given a job description in your new role, inform your manager and human resources that you should be provided with one! Also, it's important that you meet with your manager and ask him/her on what their expectations are in the role, what should your first 90 days look like, and what should be your top three to five deliverables in this role. It's critical for your success to be aligned with your manager on what good performance will look like. In addition, if you continue to be on the low scale of your pay grade, request an equity-adjustment. Good companies will give employees out-of-cycle base salary increases if your salary falls below the market range. You will only get an equity-adjustment if you ask for it.

YEAR 10
(2017)

THE YEAR STARTED with a mini-reorganization in Dave Duke's single copy area. All POC division managers (grade 15) were demoted to field supervisor (grade 14) positions. Dave created another layer of managers between them and his position. Three white division managers reported to him. I surmised that racism was an essential factor in the decision-making. One of the division managers demoted was Barack Hall, an African American who had a bachelor's degree from the University of Chicago and a Masters from Harvard University (Ivy league). Barack started in the company around the same time that Jared Trump started. Barack came from the Oakland Times, a Garrett company. While Jared was moving up the corporate ladder, Barack as a POC, was moving down the corporate ladder.

In January 2017, Mary formally rated me "exceeds standards" on my annual review. I received a 4% increase in my annual salary. My new salary was $51,246.

Table 12.0

The minimum for a job grade 16 was $49,200. The midpoint was $63,100. The maximum was $77,000.

After ten years in the company, my base salary was still equivalent to the minimum for my job grade and below the midpoint. This is extremely disappointing and a red flag for any employee, White or POC.

I disagreed with her overall assessment because I accomplished so much during my past twelve months as a first-year people manager (responsible for supervising employees). In retrospect, I exceeded all of the challenges that were given to me. I also was awarded 125% of the pay-out target for my annual incentive bonus.

However, Mary stated to me that she had never given a first-year manager an "exceptional" rating. Later, I found out that she had rated Jeff Sessions, a first-year people manager with less work experience than me, an "exceptional" in December 2016. Jeff bragged about his rating after a few beers at a Chicago Sox game we attended. Mary blatantly lied to me.

In addition, this was my first 360-degree performance review and she rated me "achieved standards" in leadership and communication. I told her that I had disagreed with the ratings. My verbal and written skills were very good. I reminded her that she did not provide me any feedback about my communication skills up to this point.

According to her, my peers did not understand the technology jargon that I used in our meetings. I reminded her that nobody has ever come to me stating that they did not understand what I was saying, including her. I also pointed out to her that only two and half months ago, she rated my leadership and communication skills exceptional.

I told her that now that I know that management does not understand the technology, I would provide a greater effort to resolve this ambiguity. Regarding the leadership rating, I reminded her that African American males are normally not perceived as leaders by white managers in this company. Also, I stated that outside of this company, I am perceived as a leader. I reminded her that customers, doctors, lawyers and successful businessmen look at me as a leader in my community, but at the Sankofa Company, I need to work on leadership? I asked her, is it leadership or is it white politics?

In February, Rudy Doyle announced another reorganization of the national, consumer delivery and single copy operations areas. Mary Cash was promoted to the newly created director of consumer distribution services. Jimmy Johns was promoted to the new director of customer development. Jeff Sessions and John McCain were promoted to a newly created customer distribution operations manager position (grade 18). Jeff, John, and Dave Duke were named the new leaders of the middle management team. Also, Billie Bob and Jared Trump (white males) received an increase in salary for inheriting some of the national markets.

Incidentally, it was no surprise that John and Jeff were promoted. Both of them were always selected for the "HiPO" or high-profile projects. They always received the highest performance ratings and merit increases. Mitch Romney loved John McCain and Jeff Sessions. Rudy Doyle also loved both of them. An all-white male clique or the good-ole-boy corporate network was alive and flourishing.

Earl Floyd and Angela Clark were the only regional managers that did not receive any increase in compensation or increase in scope of responsibility. These moves solidified the fact that African Americans were not a part of the department's long-term plans. Later in the evening, Earl told me that he and Angela knew that their days were numbered working for the Sankofa Times.

Dave Duke was then named as packaging manager in March, and Bunny Swin (white female) moved into his role as a leader on what was called the executive council (middle management team leaders). Jeff Sessions, John McCain, and Bunny met with Jimmy and Mary once a week to discuss strategies, leadership development, and day-to-day operations.

In April, Mary and Jimmy Johns requested to meet with Earl. Earl told me that they had informed him that he was going to be demoted 2-levels to a division manager (grade 15) because he did not have the skills necessary to remain as a regional manager (grade 17). They informed him to think about their decision and his external options and they would get back to him. Earl asked me to keep this strictly confidential since he was very hurt by their decision. Earl also mentioned to me that Angela requested a separation package and Mary said to her "absolutely." Earl and Angela always kept each other informed. They knew that their careers were nearly over and they would never ascend to the director-level or above a grade 17 level.

Furthermore, I knew that Mary was trying to push me and my staff into the corporate systems and technology department, so that she didn't have to deal with me anymore. The following is a letter I received from a manager from another department on my performance:

——— ◉ ———

April 3, 2017

TO: Mary Cash

FROM: Helen Byte (white female) RE: Oak Park Computer Support

A primary concern of employees at Oak Park has been lack of computer support. That has changed, dramatically with Norm Fleming. Norm and his team have not only made major changes by adding quick access to company information for all, they have also been available and willing to help whenever needed

Norm Fleming not only installed software and added more capability to my computer, he has always reacted quickly whenever a request was made, and has demonstrated competence and teamwork. In addition, although there are many demands for his expertise and time, he is always patient and ready to do what it takes to get the job done. More has been accomplished in the short time Norm has been involved, than had been accomplished in a very long time.

cc: Norm Fleming

———————

In April, Mary informed me that my new position as field technology manager would be eliminated. She stated that she was working with the corporate systems and technology to find me a position or I would remain in the publication department in another position. Furthermore, she stated that my direct reports were going to be integrated into the corporate systems and technology department.

I also had found out that Mary did not nominate me for the annual 2016 Hispanic and Black Achievers Award. I asked Mary why she did not nominate me after all of my contributions to the community. Mary stated that I did not come to her mind, so she nominated Kenneth Cantina (Hispanic) and Joe Hector (Hispanic). Hispanics were very docile in the

Company and did not leverage their strengths to challenge the status quo.

Next, Angela Clark was scheduled to go on maternity leave. Five weeks before she was scheduled to leave, Mary and Jimmy requested that I cover the Gary Region during Angela's absence. I was very disturbed about their decision. I reminded Mary that I enjoyed managing technology and that I wanted to continue to grow in the technology field. Then, I reminded her that I had applied for the corporate technology leadership development (TLDP) program on April 15th.

In addition, I informed her that I wanted to receive compensation for this additional duty. I reminded her that I was the lowest and only grade 16 in the middle management team and that I should be paid at a grade 17 or higher level.

Table 13.0

> The minimum for a job grade 17 was $55,500. The midpoint was $71,100. The maximum was $86,700.

I also asked her if she knew anything about the equity-adjustment research that was being conducted by Amy O'Conner from the compensation department. I reminded her that I had requested an equity-adjustment for my staff and myself back in March.

She stated that she had not received anything and that she would sign-off on it once she received it. I called Amy and she stated that her research was completed on our salary recommendations. She was going to send us the information the following week. After my conversation with Amy, I decided to perform both jobs.

I managed the Gary region; Division Manager Shawn Mack (white male), Division Manager Terry Easy (white male), Division Manager Ashton Clarke (African American male), Distribution Coordinator Andrew Jones (African American male). I also continued to manage the field technology group; field database manager George Slick (white male), field database Joe Hector (Hispanic male), field database Pamela Shaw (African American female) and division manager Kenneth Cantina (Hispanic male) assisted me in the day-to-day operations. I was now managing eight full-time employees.

In May, Jeff Sessions, Bunny Swin, and John McCain "asked" me if I was going to apply for the open region. I explained to all of them that I had applied for the technology leadership development program (TLDP) at the Sankofa Company in April 2017.

John asked me that if I did not get the position, then what was I going to do? He felt that I needed a contingency plan because my current position as field technology manager was slated to be eliminated. I stated to all of them that it was not my policy to apply for two positions at the same time. I did not want to mislead any of the hiring managers. Also, I reminded them that I loved technology and I wanted to continue to grow my career in technology.

I felt tremendous pressure and undue stress from all of them. I realized that I had finally started to learn a new skillset that was exciting. I did not want to go back to newspaper delivery operations. Nevertheless, on Friday, May 9th, I met with Mary to drop off my application. Mary stated that she knew my heart would not be in the position and that I should not apply for it. I agreed with her 100%. I reminded her that I would have died for the regional manager position a year ago, but my passion has now changed.

———◉———

Letter of recommendation from Mary for TLDP:

Technology Leadership Development Program

Candidate Norman Fleming

Letter recommendation by Mary Cash

I fully support Norman Fleming's application for the technology leadership development program. I have worked directly with Norm over the past sixteen months and believe he is an excellent candidate for this program. Though his undergraduate degree is in the field of business, not technology, his passion for all areas of technology should more than qualify him for the program.

Having been bitten by the techno-bug as a young man, Norm reads, studies, sleeps and breathes all facets of technology. Though a layman, he can hold his own with many individuals born and bred in the field.

Norm has been a manager at the Sankofa Times for more than six years. In the past sixteen months, he has been given two very diverse assignments to master, both of which he has done with aplomb. His most recent assignment, manager of field technology, required Norm to manage all technology requirements for the newspaper distribution network with the aid of only two other managers, neither of which had formal training in the field. This team, later joined by another technology novice, was able to install network configurations in three field offices, alleviating an ongoing communication problem while servicing all the needs of 180 contractors and 50 field managers.

Norm also was responsible for teaching many of the field managers the basic tenets of the technology he was responsible for supporting. He led many of them kicking and screaming into the age of digital communication. He held PC training seminars, Internet training and orchestrated the process of building the single copy and consumer delivery pages for the publications Intranet site.

Norm's greatest value to the technology field is his vision. He continually strives to find a better way to utilize technology. He challenges the status quo continually trying to inch ahead of the technology trends. Being a member of the technology leadership development program will give him the tools he needs to formalize that process.

In the area of basic management, Norm has excellent planning and organizational skills. He ensures that all things are completed properly in the allotted time frame. He is excellent with young managers and serves as a role model for more than one. He is active in his community and still finds time to work on his MBA at Keller Graduate School.

I feel strongly Norman Fleming would be an excellent addition to this program and would help move Sankofa forward from a highly talented and diverse perspective.

I covered the Gary region for eight weeks and did a stellar job. However, I observed racial inequities throughout this period.

First, Dave Duke was accused of harassment by an African American employee from the packaging department. It was alleged that Dave called the employee a "nigger" and physically grabbed and choked him by the neck. The employee felt physically threatened for his life.

In private, Dave told Earl that he was only suspended for ten days without pay and was not terminated. Jim O'Reilly, Steve Weisser (white), and Rudy Doyle wanted Dave to be terminated. However, Jimmy Johns and Mary Cash saved Dave as an employee and created a new position for him in the customer achievement department. Dave became the new field administration manager (grade 18). The company has a "zero-tolerance" policy against racial harassment. Obviously, this policy did not apply to Dave Duke.

Next, Earl told me that Clarence Thomas and Anna Bell from human resources did an investigation on his "pending demotion." Earl stated to me that Clarence told him that Jimmy Johns and Mary had lied to human resources. They told human resources that Earl had requested the demotion to a grade 15 position. Earl informed Clarence and Anna that he never requested the demotion.

Angela Clark officially left the company effective June 2017. She received a separation package. Furthermore, I confirmed performance problems on all three division managers from her region: Ashton, Shawn and Terry. It seemed that the only person that Mary wanted to move on was Ashton. She said that I had done a great job on documenting Ashton Clarke's (pursuing his MBA at Kellogg) performance. She stated that Angela could never articulate his problems to her. She also mentioned that Billie Bob shared the office with Angela so that he could watch Angela for her.

I forwarded documentation to Mary on performance problems reflecting all three managers. Mary Cash, Jimmy Johns, and Alma Cantina only focused on the problems that Ashton was having. On June 13th,

Ashton received a written warning on his performance deficiencies, which he deserved. Alma actually wrote Ashton's written warning for me. When I gave Ashton the written warning, he specifically asked me if we were being consistent across the region. I informed him that I was being consistent.

In addition, I forwarded performance documentation on Shawn and Terry. I received no feedback or actions from Mary, Jimmy and Alma from human resources. Shawn and Terry should have received at least a "verbal" warning on their performance problems. They received no corrective actions.

On June 22nd, Division Manager Barbi Irish (grade 15, white female) was promoted to the regional manager position (grade 17) of the Gary Region. Barbi was one of Mary's proteges. I asked Barbi if I could assist her in reviewing some of the performance issues with Shawn and Terry and Barb said no, she'd handle it.

Mike Orlando (white male) was promoted to the second regional position that was available. Charnies Clark-Ryan (African American female, grade 16) was not promoted to the regional position, even though she was the most qualified. Earl informed me that he heard that Charnise had a private meeting with Mary to discuss the decision, but Mary did not support her promotion.

In June, Jim O'Reilly, the department VP informed me that I was not chosen for the technology leadership development program (TLDP). He said that I was one of the eight finalists. He stated that they had chosen a person with extensive technology experience and a 2nd person with extensive management experience. He stated that I was right in the middle. I had a little bit of both.

He also stated that I needed to acquire broader technology experience in Sankofa systems or corporate systems and technology.

It did not surprise me, I've never received a position that I applied for at the Sankofa Times Company. This was the 23rd position I had formally applied for during my 10-year career with the Sankofa Times, and of course, I was not selected.

What was disturbing was the fact that the hiring criteria had changed. At first, in the interviews with Jim and Jeff Apple (white male), chief technology officer for Sankofa Company, they stated that they were not looking for people with extensive technology or management experience. They stated that they were looking for a combination of both. They wanted people who had the aptitude to learn technology and management. Also, the program had four positions open, and they only filled two.

Consequently, this is how the Sankofa Times invisibly limits promotional opportunities for POCs; they always change the criteria during the interview process.

I informed Jimmy Johns and Mary Cash that I did not receive the position. Jimmy stated to not worry about it, that they had plenty of work for me to do in the customer achievement function. Mary said that she would talk to Karen McBrien, director of systems and technology, about positions in her department. I informed Mary that I wanted to get broader technology experience and she should look in the corporate systems department. Mary did not seem to care about me. She seemed bothered that I was not leaving her department.

In July, the middle management team completed its salary planning for 2018. There were thirty-three managers in professional job grades 15 through 16. Three out of the thirty-three positions were job grades 16. Corporate Account Manager, Brian Peer was making $57,613, Senior Operations Manager, Thomas Maple was making $72,898, and I was making $51,246. My salary ranked number 12 out of 33 employees; there were nine division managers in a lower grade that made more money than I did.

Table 14.0

In the FY2018 Merit Planning Guide, the minimum for a job grade 16 was $50,676. The midpoint was $64,993. The maximum was $79,310.

I noticed that NOT only was I the lowest paid in my job grade 16, but the four African American grade fifteen managers were in the bottom 25% quartile; Pamela Shaw ranked 27, Yvette Johnson ranked 24, Ashton Clarke ranked 30, and Charles Cubs ranked 33 (lowest salary).

My analysis forced me to continue to push the equity-adjustment issue with Mary. Incidentally, during the meeting, Mary recommended that Terry Easy rated "exceeds standards" for his 2017 performance. Terry was a good-ole-boy.

———◈———

Letter I developed in July 2017

MEMO TO FILE

FROM: NORMAN P. FLEMING

RE: EQUITY ADJUSTMENT REQUEST

On Thursday, March 6, 2017, Regional Managers John McCain and Billie Bob informed me that my field technology group would be eliminated from the annual incentive program for managers. There was speculation that my area was going to be absorbed by the corporate systems & technology division. Also, they stated that sales incentives were not given to technology employees. Billie suggested that I speak to planning & analysis director Jay Cutler, to find out the steps that I would need to follow for an equity-adjustment on salaries.

I confirmed my plans for the equity-adjustment with my supervisor, Mary Cash. On March 9th, I sent an e-mail to Jay Cutler requesting information on the procedures for an equity adjustment. Jay replied with his thoughts and suggested that I speak to Jana Baze from human resources.

I spoke to Jana and she recommended that I speck to Rejjie Russ from the human resources area located at the corporate center. Later, I called Rejjie and she recommended that I speak to Amy O'Conner from the compensation area in human resources. I forwarded my original e-mail message detailing my objectives to Amy. Then I called her. She acknowledged my e-mail and informed me that she would do a thorough research on the compensation equity between my area and similar positions in the systems & technology division.

I met with Mary Cash inquiring about the status of the equity adjustment for my area. She stated that she had not received anything from Amy O'Conner. In addition, she assured me that she would sign-off on her recommendations. After our meeting, I called Amy and asked her about the status of her research. Amy stated that she did complete the research and that she would forward to me the results on my staff and my position to Mary next week. On April 18th, I sent her an e-mail to confirm our discussion.

I asked Mary if she had received any information on the equity-adjustment for my area. She stated that she had not received anything from Amy. I left a message on Amy's telephone mailbox requesting her to forward her research to Mary. Amy never called me to confirm my request.

Later in the week, I asked Mary if she had received any information on the equity-adjustment. She stated that she had not received anything. On May 14th, I sent Amy an e-mail requesting her to forward her recommendations to Mary. Amy did not reply to my e-mail or call my office.

I left a phone mail message for Amy to call me. She never called me. On May 20th, I again called Amy. She stated that she was going to fax the researched results to Mary after her conversation with me. On May 21st, I saw Mary and asked her if she had received the equity information from Amy. Mary stated that she did receive the information.

I met with Mary and asked her if she had signed-off on the equity-adjustment. She stated that she had forwarded the information to Jim O'Reilly, but he had questions about the request. In addition, she stated that Jim did not know anything about her plans to integrate my area into the corporate systems & technology division. Also, she stated that she was waiting to find out if I was going to receive the associate position for the technology leadership development program that I applied for on April 15th.

I informed her that I was not chosen for the technology leadership development program. I was one of the eight finalists. Four positions were open, but only two people were accepted into the program.

It is now July 16th, 132 days since I've presented my request, and I still do not know anything about the results of the equity-adjustment research. I should have at least received the results on the three managers that directly report to me. As an employee, all I expected was due diligence, integrity, and simple follow-through from the people that were responsible for my request.

At this moment, I am extremely disappointed with this process and discouraged about the adverse treatment toward loyal and "high-potential" employees. A simple, "Norm, we are not going to approve the equity-adjustment" would have been acceptable. I can live with honesty and direct communication, but I should not be expected to ignore practices that adversely affect my life and well-being.

Sincerely, Norman Fleming

———◎———

In August, after pursuing the equity-adjustment for more than five months, I realized that Mary was evading the issue and me. Senior Analyst Tom Long (white) informed me that the process only took them two months when Jay Cutler did it for his analysts. Tom stated that his base-salary was increased to the operation's analyst's average (midpoint) compensation level and his annual division manager bonus was also rolled into his salary. Furthermore, seven division managers were given an equity adjustment in May 2017. Jeff Sessions (grade 18) and John McCain (grade 18) also received out-of-cycle equity-adjustments in February 2017. Both of their salaries were increased to $90,000 per year.

Table 15.0

The minimum for a job grade 18 was $61,500. The midpoint was $78,800. The maximum was $96,100.

Jeff and John both started their careers straight out of college and had three years less work experience than I did. Their annual base salary was $90,000 per year (near the maximum) while my base salary was only $51,246 per year (near the minimum). How did they make $38,754 or 76% more a year than I did? What did I do wrong as a POC?

I finally met with Mary on July 29th, and she informed me that she was waiting for Karen McBrien (director of systems & technology) to make a decision on our future positions. I stated to her that Karen McBrien's decision should not change the fact that my staff and myself will no longer be eligible to receive an annual bonus. In addition, I reminded her that I would like to have seen the research completed on my direct reports. She asked me how much I thought my salary should be. I told her that my salary should be more than $60,000 per year. She stated to me that no regional manager (grade 17) made more than $60,000 per year.

Table 16.0

The minimum for a job grade 17 was $55,500. The midpoint was $71,100. The maximum was $86,700.

At this point, I knew that she was lying again. Mary stated that she would talk to Vince Carmucci, our new vice president, about it on Friday, August 1st.

On Monday, August 4th, Mary sent me an e-mail stating that she wanted to meet with me on Wednesday, August 6th, to discuss three issues. One of the issues was about my communication with Amy Trump (white female). After I received her e-mail, I immediately went to her office and asked why "Amy" was on the agenda for Wednesday. Mary stated that I have a communication problem and Amy is an example of my problem. She stated that I only communicate through e-mail and I never pick-up the phone to speak to people. I interjected and told Mary that I disagreed with her assessment. Then she stated that Lisa Kapper (Amy's white boss) called her and sent her an email in which Amy called me a bitter old man. I told Mary that I am not going to accept this treatment from Amy.

On Wednesday, August 6th, Mary stated that she wanted to change our meeting time from 8:00 am to 9:00 am so that Jimmy Johns could attend. I entered Mary's office at 9:00 am and she seemed to be upset. She asked me if I felt that I've been discriminated against and I told her Yes, that for nine and a half years I've felt that diversity did not include African American males in the Sankofa Times Company. She then stated that I would need to meet with human resources after our meeting so the company could prepare to defend itself against a lawsuit from me. I told her that I loved the Sankofa Times and had no plans to sue the company.

Jim entered the office and we talked about the issues. I explained to them how I've felt about my experience with the company for more than nine years. I stated that the Sankofa Times does a very poor job in promoting, retaining and compensating high-potential POC managers. I reminded them that African American males must always prove themselves before they're given promotional opportunities. I stated that my only promotion in more than six years was not given to me until after I worked in the position as a "special project." Mary immediately looked at me and said that I was fibbing.

I looked at Mary and reminded her that my promotion was not official until six weeks after performing in the position. In addition, I stated that I had never been promoted to a position that I had formally applied for through the company job-posting process. I also stated that 95% of the African American males that started with me in 2008 are no longer here in the company.

Jim and Mary wanted me to think about what I wanted to do (field technology, corporate, customer achievement, or systems and technology) and they stated that they would help me.

Jim alluded that my interpersonal skills were not the best, but that was not always important because Jerry Jones did not have strong interpersonal skills. I stated to Jim and Mary that I did not want to be treated differently from the other managers. Jim stated that it was okay to receive assistance and support because managers are always receiving assistance from other managers.

They asked me if I was upset because I did not get the TLDP position. I told them No. I stated that when I submitted my application, I did not believe that the Sankofa Company would select an African American male to a key leadership position. Jim stated that I was rated one of the top managers in planning, organization, and control.

Then they asked me why I didn't apply for the open regional positions after John McCain and Jeff Sessions told me to apply. I corrected them, and told them that Jeff and John did not tell me to apply; they asked me if I was going to apply. Mary and Jim looked at each other and said that they were given the wrong information. I reminded Mary that I was going to apply, but she and I agreed that my heart would not be in it. I reminded them that my heart was in technology and I wanted to continue to learn.

If they had asked me this question a year ago, I would have been thrilled about applying for the regional position. Mary stated that she was going to meet with Karen McBrien to discuss the future of the field technology group. She felt that there was still work in her area for my people to do. Finally, we all agreed to reconvene at a later date to discuss this further.

Later, I met with Alma Cantina from human resources. She stated that she had sent my EEO Complaint letter to other human resources and legal managers. We discussed the same issues that I had discussed with Mary and Jim. Alma was also displaying her desire to help me find a position in technology. I reminded Alma that I only had one year of technology experience and it is very difficult to move in this company with one year. In addition, I stated to her that I've been troubled since March, because my position was going to be eliminated and there was no movement on the equity-adjustment.

I stated that it was very odd that I never received the report on the equity adjustment recommendations for my direct reports. Also, I stated that when I was given the position, Mary told me that my position would grow with increasing responsibility and direct reports. I was given three employees with no experience, a $62,000 annual capital/expense budget, and no full authority or control of the distribution technologies my team supported.

Furthermore, I stated to Alma that Jimmy and Mary now want to help me find a niche. But they should have come to me a month ago after I told them that I was not accepted in the technology leadership development program. Also, I stated to her that I hope they do not ostracize me.

She asked me if I felt that I've been discriminated against. I told her Yes. I stated that during my nine and a half years of employment, I'd been a victim of subtle discrimination. The discrimination limits and hinders promotional opportunities for myself and other African American males. Also, I stated that there was a disparity in compensation between Whites and African Americans. I told her that human resources has all of the data and information on the disparity between African Americans and white males. I suggested to her to look into their database and review some of the same trends that I have noticed over the years. Alma stated that she would like to reconvene the following week so that we could discuss my issues further.

On August 14th, I met again with Alma. I stated to her that I did not trust the company and that I needed more time to decide on the path that I needed to take. During our conversation, she told me that

Mary told "me" that she was going to keep our positions in her department. Surprised, I told Alma that Mary never directly told me that I was staying in the department. Mary told me that she was "going to talk to Karen McBrien" because she felt that they still needed us in her area.

However, she never stated to me that "I was staying in her area." Alma looked confused and stated that this is what Mary told her the day after our meeting. I responded to Alma and stated that this is another example of miscommunication. I stated to Alma that I was contemplating resigning from the company because of the lack of compensation and opportunities. She stated that maybe Mary was going to forward the equity-adjustment next week. Then she wanted me to provide her with more specifics on my assessment of discrimination. I stated to her that I needed more time and that she probably had access to more information than I did. She ended the meeting by stating that she would touch base with me in two weeks.

Later on in the day, Alma privately came into my

office and stated that she hoped that I would not resign from the company.

Next, I met with Michelle Rusty (African American female) from human resources and reviewed my official "employee personnel" file. There were no negative documents inside the entire file. The file had all of my official annual performance reviews, internal job applications, salary change forms, benefits information, and miscellaneous documents.

At the end of August, my technology team was officially transferred to the corporate systems & technology team under Karen McBrien. My base salary was adjusted and my annual sales bonus of 10% a year was now rolled into my new base salary. Corporate systems or non-sales employees were not eligible for annual bonuses. My new total compensation with no bonus was now $68,060 per year.

My new direct manager was Jeff Russia (white male, grade 17). After three years as a part-time student, I also graduated Magna Cum Laude with my MBA in information systems.

My full-time position was eliminated after the transfer to corporate.

One month later, I received an offer, accepted it, and was promoted to a directorship position (equivalent to a grade 21 level) at a major competitor in the same industry. My annual base salary increased from $68,060 to $98,000 (+44%), then to a $115,000 annual base after six months of performance on the job; a whopping 69% increase in annual base salary.

Table 17.0

Compared to the Sankofa Times, the minimum for my new job grade 21 was $87,500. The midpoint was $112,200. The maximum was $136,900.

For the first time in my career, my base salary was higher than the company's job grade midpoint. Also, my scope of responsibilities increased to managing people managers and a staff of twenty full-time employees. Also, I was eligible for an annual bonus of 15%, plus stock options. My total compensation potential more than tripled in less than a 1-year period to $210,000 per year.

FY2017 CONCLUSIONS – LESSONS LEARNED:

- Corporate America: Honesty, transparency, and integrity goes a long way in attracting, developing, and retaining POCs. POCs will not always win the extra points in political branding and relationships. Don't change the rules of engagement on internal promotions and transfers. Don't put yourself in a position where there is circumstantial discrimination or retaliation. You will not optimize your success if POCs are the lowest paid employees with the highest rate of turnover. It may cost you over $100k a year in recruiting costs to replace one qualified POC manager.

- People of Color: You behaved as your authentic self. You maintained your performance at a high level. You pursued developmental assignments. You collaborated with employees. You were rewarded with a better opportunity outside of your company. Your experience, education, and potential "finally" paid off at a better company. Congratulations on the well-deserved promotion. You have now achieved your Market Value!

FINAL THOUGHTS

WHAT IS DISCRIMINATION in corporate America?

Discrimination occurs when an employee or group of employees are treated less favorably than similarly situated employees of a different race, sex, age, national origin, religion, etc. The difference in treatment can be either blatant, such as, jokes, slurs, and innuendoes, or subtle, such as job assignments, training, and promotions. The Sankofa Times tends to be of the subtle form.

After ten years of enjoying incremental career success, awesome colleagues, internal recognition and achievement, I had also suffered from depression, migraine headaches, and unfair treatment. I've concluded that certain Sankofa Times people managers did not consistently adhere to its equal employment opportunity policy and federal and state laws.

Listed below are the results of the Sankofa Times's POC professional grade representation metrics in fiscal year 2016:

The publications department had around 1,600 part-time and full-time grades 1 to 22 employees toward the end of 2016. POCs account for most of the lower-paid positions that fell on the scale of non-professional (grades 1 to 11), i.e., customer service representatives, data-entry clerks, inside sales, packaging helpers, janitors, etc.

There were approximately 250 full-time employees within the professional grades 12 to 22 levels in the department. There were only seven (2.8%) POCs at the end of 2016 in the entire publications department that were at job grade 15 or above. Only two out of the seven POCs were at a grade 17 or above. These are unacceptable numbers. POC metrics matters in business or you will not stay in business for long.

Moving forward, I hope *your company* will continue to leverage or implement the following TEN leading D&I practices:

1) D&I Leadership starts at the Top (C-Level executives), but behaviors must trickle throughout the company. Hold every employee accountable to your D&I values and expectations.

   a. POCs: Bring your best every day to your job. Be your authentic self and realize performance matters. You must commit to becoming a high performer with high potential in your career endeavors.

2) Seek first to understand diversity risks and legal matters. Don't just jump to one-way investigations and preparing for a legal defense. It's a lot cheaper to correct an isolated internal issue than to fight a $300 million-dollar class-action lawsuit. And don't defend bad managers that lack the skillset to embrace a diverse workforce.

    a. POCs: Document, document, and document any inconsistencies you notice in the way you are treated and managed. Leverage your Human Resources contacts, Code of Conduct policies, and feel safe to Speak Up.

3) Get rid of the naysayers and employees that do not buy into the company's long-term vision on D&I. You have a zero-tolerance policy for one primary reason—to keep you out of jail.

    a. POCs: Always be honest and truthful in any internal investigation on EEO complaints. Facts should always prevail in an investigation.

4) Pay for performance and drive balance and equity for all employees. If you don't pay a certain protected group fairly, you will lose them to your competitor. And you will lose your business to your competitors.

    a. POCs: If you are underpaid, you have two choices. Stay or leave for better pay.

If you don't ask for an equity-adjustment, then no one else in the company will ask on your behalf.

5) Ensure your company's leadership development programs are open to all employees and lead by example. Lead with "inclusion" as a weighted acceptance criterion for White and POCs.

    a. POCs: Volunteer to facilitate an internal training program. Make sure inclusion is always your focus area. White and POC careers all matter.

6) Benchmark your D&I practices against other companies and always focus on continuous improvement. Create an Executive-level Diversity & Inclusion council and invite C-Level leaders from other top-tier companies. Aspire to become the D&I leader in your industry. Measure your D&I maturity level every year and communicate in your Annual Financial report.

a. POCs: If you're an external hire, bring best-of-breed D&I practices from your previous employer. Volunteer and lead an employee resource group (ERG). ERGs will provide you visibility and access to senior leaders.

7) Tie D&I targets to every employees' goals, incentives, and long-term stock awards. If you don't measure D&I, you can't monitor D&I, and then, you can't manage D&I outcomes.

a. POCs: Make sure your annual performance goals are SMART (Specific, Measurable, Attainable, Reasonable, and Timebound). Add your D&I accomplishments in your performance self-review submission.

8) Eliminate the internal and external "ghost" promotion practices and succession plans that are only filled with white males and never posted for POCs. All employees should know what the hiring criteria is, and hiring managers should

stick to it. You should post 100% of all open positions. There is no place for personal biases and bad promotions should not be tolerated.

    a. POCs: Always prepare and bring your best to an interview. After you complete your interview(s), always send a personal thank you email to the interview team and hiring manager. And, if you're not selected, always ask for feedback from the hiring manager on what you can do better for the next opportunity.

9) Promote D&I quick wins and annual recognition on your public web site and via press releases to your investors. You will outperform your competitors by leading with the best authentic talent on the globe.

    a. POCs: Help promote your company's diversity wins. Always be willing to volunteer and participate in photo opportunities. Great leaders value employees that are engaged and champions of the company.

10)   Actively participate in community events and activities for all employees. Your diverse employee base should serve all diverse communities, not just the ones that look like one race.

  a. POCs: Be willing to participate in all community events. Don't just focus on the POC community events. Be open and willing to lead non-POC events. We now live in a global society with employees from every country and ethnicity.

Finally, I hope you enjoyed my story and I pray you've embraced these leading practices in diversity & inclusion. And, I hope *you* are committed to bringing these practices back to your company. Let's **"Make America Hope Again."**

ABOUT THE AUTHOR

Norman P. Fleming has over 30 years of professional business experience in corporate America. He is the founder and president of Fleming Consulting LLC. He was a senior director of Enterprise Business Solutions, at MillerCoors USA, senior director of IT Client Relationship Management at Astellas Pharma, director of Client Services at The New York Times Company, manager of Program Integration & Management at Deloitte Consulting, manager of Global IT for the Global Human Health division at Merck, manager of Business Systems at Kraft Heinz Foods company, Remote Systems Support supervisor at the Chicago Tribune Company, Store manager at Payless Shoesource, and served his country as a member of the Illinois Army National Guard.

Mr. Fleming is a recipient of the 2017 Albert Nelson Marquis Lifetime Achievement Award in Science & Engineering, 2014 Outstanding MBA of the Year for the National Black MBA Association, 2014 DiversityMBA Magazine's Top 100 Executives Under 50 Achievement Award, 2014 DeVry University's Distinguished MBA Alumni Achievement Award, 2013 National BDPA Epsilon & Corporate Champion Award, and recognized by the International Who's Who in Professional Management in 2000.

The author lived in Midtown Manhattan (NYC), Philadelphia, and currently lives in Chicago where he enjoys watching major league sports, traveling to the Caribbean, mentoring at-risk youths, and spending quality time with family and friends. He is also an active member of Alpha Phi Alpha Fraternity, Inc., IT Senior Management Forum, Project Management Institute, and the 100 Black Men of Chicago.

He received his Bachelor of Science degree in Management from Southern Illinois University at Carbondale and an MBA in Information Systems from DeVry University, Keller Graduate School of Management.

ACKNOWLEDGEMENTS

I would like to personally thank the following mentors and friends that have inspired me and made a positive impact on shaping my professional life:

Angela R. Clark, Shawn K. Moore, Dr. Sydney Jordan, Charles Levy, Randy Hulskotter, Steve Canty, Eric Bieronski, Nila M. Bieronski, Kenneth Nash, Eugene Childs, Kenneth Harris, Harvey Keith Porchia, Cheryl Brewer, Charles Dockery, Steve Keane, David Diedrich, Donnell Knighten, Kenneth Santiago, Frank Gihan, Willie Fields, Benjamin Peoples, Michael G. Williams, Scott Heekin-Canedy, Sandra Schirmang, Barry Peters, Kwame Salter, George Llado, Troy Drayton, Dr. Walter Kimble, Marc Portner, John Kendall, Parish Ivy, Anthony Bennett, Reggie Marsh, Steven Broaden,

Aaron Young, Kathy Motes, Steve Poquette, Ladan Saeid, Carmen Giles, Jadonal Ford, Jeff Jackson, Sharron Troupe, Melodi Warren-Anderson, Terri Lambe, Earl A. Pace, Jr., Michael A. Williams, Steve Canal, Allen Baylor, Robert McMillian, Kenneth Watkins, Jr., Isiah Ward, Charles Jones, Sr., Louis Fields, Lori Powell, Denise Thomas, Wendell Corbin, Ron Cureton, George Walker, Jose Cruz, Rory Woodfaulk, Rudy Rodriguez, Ronnie Watson, Archie Wesley, Lester McCarroll, Undray Wilkes, James Norman, Kimberly Shelby, Mike Mayo, Brad Neilly, Jamie Scott Rieger, Keisha Williams-Banks, Jaideep Mukherjee, Angela Foster-Woods, Spencer Palmer, Kathy April-Rush, David A. Day, Royce Willis, Pat E. Perkins, Kaplan Mobray, Aaron Martinez, Earl Wheatfall, Mark Tillman, Darryl R. Matthews, Sr., John M. Williams, Royce Wills, Mark Fuller, Vince Adams, John McClendon, Shun Dyes, Roland S. Martin, Adarious Payton, Rajeev Vasudeva, Ryan Clark, Ashton L. Clark, Juan Thomas, Thelma Rocio, Marvin Miller, Fernando Clark, Keenan Wilborn, Kathy Clark, Gina Billings, Monique Berry, and Joyce Perry.

CPSIA information can be obtained
at www.ICGtesting.com
Printed in the USA
BVHW01s2024271117

501320BV00020B/659/P